Pizza and Focaccia

ACADEMIA
BARILLA

The Taunton Press

ACADEMIA BARILLA
AMBASSADOR OF ITALIAN GASTRONOMY
THROUGHOUT THE WORLD

Academia Barilla is a global movement toward the protection, development and promotion of authentic regional Italian culture and cuisine.
With the concept of Food as Culture at our core, Academia Barilla offers a 360° view of Italy. Our comprehensive approach includes:

- a state-of-the-art culinary center in Parma, Italy;
- gourmet travel programs and hands-on cooking classes;
- the world's largest Italian gastronomic library and historic menu collection;
- a portfolio of premium artisan food products;
- global culinary certification programs;
- custom corporate services and training;
- team building activities;
- and a vast assortment of Italian cookbooks.

Thank you and we look forward to welcoming you in Italy soon!

CONTENTS

EDITED BY
ACADEMIA BARILLA

PHOTOGRAPHS
ALBERTO ROSSI

RECIPES BY
CHEF MARIO GRAZIA
CHEF LUCA ZANGA

TEXT BY
MARIAGRAZIA VILLA

ACADEMIA BARILLA EDITORIAL COORDINATION
CHATO MORANDI
ILARIA ROSSI
REBECCA PICKRELL

GRAPHIC DESIGN
PAOLA PIACCO

On the whole, the pizza must be soft, elastic, and easily foldable in half to form a "libretto." [...] soft to the touch and to the mouth...

DRAFT LAW LAYING DOWN RULES TO PROTECT REAL NEAPOLITAN PIZZA, 2004

PIZZA

Pizza is an extremely simple yet clever invention—colorful and convivial. It is also fragrant, enticing, and tasty. Only a century ago, pizza was a specialty you could only savor in Naples, but today it is Italy's most famous gastronomical specialty, enjoyed around the world.

This book collects 40 traditional Italian recipes for pizza and focaccia, carefully selected by Academia Barilla, an international center dedicated to the promotion of Italian gastronomy. Some, like the classic Margherita or Marinara, are veritable flagships of the peninsula's cuisine. Others showcase great Italian products: flavorful Parma ham; blue cheese and Sicilian provolone; Pachino tomatoes and porcini mushrooms.

The name "pizza" actually precedes by centuries the tomato pizza as we know it. The word evolved from the work of a *pistor*, Latin for baker. Although the tomato reached Naples at the end of the 16th century, it was not part of the cuisine until the 18th century, when pizza became popular across class boundaries. It is said that in 1762 the Bourbon King Ferdinand IV went to a Neapolitan pizzeria to try this simple food and was so impressed that he described it as a delicious dish. The pizza *alla marinara*, or the seafarer's pizza, has a topping of only tomatoes, oil, garlic, and oregano, ingredients that could be kept fresh onboard a ship without deteriorating.

The origin of the best-known pizza in the world, the *pizza Margherita*, however, is well known. In June 1889, Umberto I and Queen Margherita spent their summer holidays in the royal palace of Capodimonte. Tired of the usual sophisticated cuisine, they decided to try the popular bread dish. They summoned to court the most famous Neapolitan *pizzaiolo*, or pizza cook, Raffaele Esposito, who, together with his wife, prepared three pizzas: One traditional, with lard, cheese, and basil; another topped with garlic, oil, and tomato; and a third, especially created for the occasion with tomato, mozzarella, and basil representing the colors of the Italian flag. This the queen particularly liked, so don Raffaele called it Margherita in her honor.

Pizza can be thick or thin, crunchy or soft, frugal or rich. The true Neapolitan pizza has a spongy dough and has slightly thicker edges to prevent the topping from sliding off. But toppings should be genuine ingredients: fleshy olives, tasty anchovies, succulent provola cheese and sweet San Marzano cherry tomatoes. It is best cooked in a wood-fired oven and eaten folded in four, and by hand.

PISSALADIERA

Preparation time: 20 minutes   Rising time: 1 hour 10 minutes-4 hours
Cooking time: 30 minutes   Difficulty: medium

4 SERVINGS

FOR THE DOUGH
5 cups (650 g) **all-purpose flour** or
Italian "00" flour, plus more as needed
1 1/2 cups (350 ml) **lukewarm water**
1/2 oz. (15 g) **active dry yeast**
2 1/2 tsp. (15 g) **salt**

FOR THE TOPPING
2 cups (500 g) **crushed tomatoes**

11 oz. (300 g) **onions**, thinly sliced
3 1/2 oz. (100 g) **taggiasca** or other
small black olives
1 **small bunch of basil**
10 **anchovy fillets in salt**
4 cloves **garlic**
Chopped fresh oregano
2 tbsp. (30 ml) **extra-virgin olive oil**
Salt

Put the flour onto a clean work surface and make a well in the center. Dissolve
the yeast in the water. Pour the yeast mixture into the well, gradually start
incorporating it into the flour until a loose dough starts to form, then add the
salt. Knead the dough until smooth and elastic.

Cover the dough with a kitchen towel and let rise in a warm place until it has
doubled in volume (it can take from 1 to 4 hours, depending on the temperature).
Roll out the dough on an oiled pizza pan or baking tray and let it rise again for
about 10 minutes.

Sauté the onions over low heat in a pan with the olive oil. Add the anchovy fillets
and crushed tomatoes. Cook for 5 to 10 minutes and then add the basil.
Alternatively, you can add the basil when you remove the pizza from the overn.
Let the sauce cool and then spread it over the dough, garnish with olives, and
sprinkle with oregano and salt.

Bake in the oven at 375°F (190°C) for 30 minutes, or until golden brown.

ARTICHOKE PIZZA

Preparation time: 15 minutes   Rising time: 1 1/2 hours–6 hours
Cooking time: 20 minutes   Difficulty: medium

4 SERVINGS

FOR THE DOUGH
4 cups (500 g) **all-purpose flour** or
Italian "00" flour, plus more as needed
1 1/2 cups (350 ml) **lukewarm water**
1 1/2 tbsp. (20 ml) **extra-virgin olive oil**
1 1/2 tsp. (4 g) **active dry yeast** for
2-hour rising time, or 3/4 tsp. (2 g)
for 6-hour rising time

2 tsp. (12 g) **salt**

FOR THE TOPPING
1 16-oz. can **peeled tomatoes**, crushed
by hand
14 oz. (400 g) **fresh mozzarella cheese**,
sliced
15 **artichoke hearts in oil**

Put the flour onto a clean work surface and make a well in the center. Dissolve the
yeast in the water, and pour the yeast mixture into the well. Gradually start
incorporating the yeast mixture into the flour until a loose dough starts to form,
then add the oil and salt. Knead the dough until smooth and elastic. Rub the
dough with a little oil, cover with plastic wrap, and let it rest for about 10 minutes.
Grease a 12-inch round pizza pan with oil. Transfer the dough to the pan and,
using your fingertips, spread the dough to cover the bottom of the pan.
If you used 1 1/2 tsp. yeast, let the dough rise for about 40 minutes. If you used
3/4 tsp., cover the dough with a sheet of lightly oiled plastic wrap and refrigerate
for at least 5 hours. The dough will rise well in the refrigerator, becoming light
and fragrant. When the dough has risen, spread the tomatoes over the surface,
then arrange the mozzarella and the artichoke hearts (all at room temperature)
on top. Let the dough rise for another 40 minutes. Bake in the oven at 425°F
(220°C) for 20 minutes, or until the crust is golden brown.

PIZZA WITH PEPPERS

Preparation time: 30 minutes   Rising time: 1 1/2 hours–5 1/2 hours
Cooking time: 8 minutes   Difficulty: easy

4 SERVINGS

FOR THE DOUGH	FOR THE TOPPING

FOR THE DOUGH
5 cups (650 g) **all-purpose flour** or
Italian "00" flour, plus more as needed
3/4 tsp. (2 g) **active dry yeast**
1 1/2 cups plus 1 tsp. (375 ml)
lukewarm water
1 tbsp. (18 g) **salt**

FOR THE TOPPING
1 1/3 lbs. (600 g) **crushed tomatoes**
1 lb. (500 g) **fresh mozzarella**, shredded
1 1/3 lbs. (600 g) **green, red or yellow
bell peppers**
1/2 bunch **fresh basil leaves**, chopped
Salt
Extra-virgin olive oil

Put the flour onto a clean work surface and make a well in the center. Dissolve the yeast in the water, and gradually incorporate it into the flour until a loose dough forms; add the salt. Knead the dough until smooth. Cover with lightly oiled plastic; let rise until doubled in volume (from 1 to 4 hours, depending on the temperature). Divide the dough into four portions, roll them into balls and let them rise again until doubled in size (from 30 minutes to 1 hour, depending on the temperature).

Roast peppers at 390°F (200°C) until browned and tender, 15 to 20 minutes. Transfer to a bowl, cover with plastic wrap and cool. Peel, core and seed peppers and cut lengthwise into quarters. Season tomatoes salt and a drizzle of olive oil. On a floured surface, flatten each dough ball, starting with your fingertips and progressing to a rotary movement of your hands as the dough gets flatter and wider, into a round about 8 inches in diameter.

Put the dough rounds on a baking sheet. Spread each with crushed tomato, mozzarella and peppers. Bake at 480°F (250°C) for 8 minutes, or until the cheese is bubbly and the crust is golden brown. Garnish with basil.

FOUR-SEASONS PIZZA

Preparation time: 15 minutes   Rising time: 1 1/2–6 hours
Cooking time: 20 minutes   Difficulty: medium

4 SERVINGS

FOR THE DOUGH

4 cups (500 g) **all-purpose flour** or
Italian "00" flour, plus more as needed
1 1/2 cups (350 ml) **lukewarm water**
1 1/2 tbsp. (20 ml) **extra-virgin olive oil**
1 1/2 tsp. (4 g) **active dry yeast** for
2-hour rising time, or 3/4 tsp. (2 g)
for 6-hour rising time
2 tsp. (12 g) **salt**

FOR THE TOPPING

1 16-oz. can **peeled tomatoes**,
crushed by hand
14 oz. (400 g) **mozzarella cheese**,
shredded
10 **artichoke hearts in oil**
6 **button mushrooms**, sliced
10 **green olives**, pitted
6 **ham slices**

Put the flour onto a clean work surface and make a well in the center. Dissolve the yeast in the water. Gradually incorporate the yeast mixture into the flour until a loose dough forms, then add the oil and salt. Knead the dough until smooth and elastic. Rub the dough with a little oil, cover with plastic wrap, and let it rest for about 10 minutes. Grease a 12-inch round pizza pan with oil. Using your fingertips, spread the dough to cover the bottom of the pan.

If you used 1 1/2 tsp. of yeast, let the dough rise for about 40 minutes. If you used 3/4 tsp., then cover the dough with a sheet of lightly oiled plastic wrap and refrigerate for at least 5 hours. The dough will rise perfectly well in the refrigerator, becoming light and fragrant. When the dough has risen, spread the tomatoes over surface, and then arrange mozzarella, artichoke hearts, sliced mushrooms and olives (at room temperature) on top. Let the dough rise for 40 minutes. Bake at 425°F (220°C) for 18 minutes. Add the ham (at room temperature) and bake for 2 to 3 more minutes, or until cheese is bubbly and crust is golden brown.

FOUR-CHEESE PIZZA

Preparation time: 15 minutes   Rising time: 1 1/2–6 hours
Cooking time: 20 minutes   Difficulty: medium

4 SERVINGS

FOR THE DOUGH
4 cups (500 g) **all-purpose flour** or
Italian "00" flour, plus more as needed
1 1/2 cups (350 ml) **lukewarm water**
1 1/2 tbsp. (20 ml) **extra-virgin olive oil**
1 1/2 tsp. (4 g) **active dry yeast** for
2-hour rising time, or 3/4 tsp. (2 g)
for 6-hour rising time
2 tsp. (12 g) **salt**

FOR THE TOPPING
1 16-oz. can **peeled tomatoes**, crushed
by hand
3 1/2 oz. (100 g) **Gorgonzola cheese**,
crumbled
3 1/2 oz. (100 g) **Fontina cheese**, shredded
3 1/2 oz. (100 g) **Brie**, diced
3 1/2 oz. (100 g) **smoked Scamorza** or
mozzarella cheese, shredded

Put the flour onto a clean work surface and make a well in the center. Dissolve the yeast in the water, and pour the yeast mixture into the well. Gradually start incorporating the yeast mixture into the flour until a loose dough starts to form, then add the oil and salt. Knead the dough until smooth and elastic. Rub the dough with a little oil, cover with plastic wrap, and let it rest for about 10 minutes Grease a 12-inch round pizza pan with oil. Transfer the dough to the pan and, using your fingertips, spread the dough to cover the bottom of the pan.
If you used 1 1/2 tsp. of yeast, let the dough rise for about 40 minutes. If, on the other hand, you used 3/4 tsp., then cover the dough with a sheet of lightly oiled plastic wrap and refrigerate for at least 5 hours. The dough will rise well in the refrigerator, becoming light and fragrant.
When the dough has risen, top with tomatoes. Sprinkle with the cheeses. Let the dough rise for 40 minutes more and bake at 425°F (220°C) for 20 minutes, or until the cheese is bubbly and the crust is golden brown.

GORGONZOLA PIZZA

Preparation time: 15 minutes   Rising time: 1 1/2–6 hours
Cooking time: 20 minutes   Difficulty: medium

4 SERVINGS

FOR THE DOUGH
4 cups (500 g) **all-purpose flour** or
Italian "00" flour, plus more as needed
1 1/2 cups (350 ml) **water**
1 1/2 tbsp. (20 ml) **extra-virgin olive oil**
1 1/2 tsp. (4 g) **active dry yeast** for
2-hour rising time, or 3/4 tsp. (2 g)
for 6-hour rising time

2 tsp. (12 g) **salt**

FOR THE TOPPING
1 16-oz. can **peeled tomatoes**, crushed
by hand
4 1/4 oz. (150 g) **Gorgonzola cheese**,
diced
20 **walnuts**, chopped

Put the flour onto a clean work surface and make a well in the center. Dissolve the yeast in the water, and pour the yeast mixture into the well. Gradually start incorporating the yeast mixture into the flour until a loose dough starts to form, then add the oil and salt. Knead the dough until smooth and elastic. Rub the dough with a little oil, cover with plastic wrap, and let it rest for about 10 minutes. Grease a 12-inch round pizza pan with oil. Transfer the dough to the pan and, using your fingertips, spread the dough to cover the bottom of the pan.
If you used 1 1/2 tsp. of yeast, let the dough rise for about 40 minutes. If, on the other hand, you used 3/4 tsp., then cover the dough with a sheet of lightly oiled plastic wrap and refrigerate for at least 5 hours. The dough will rise perfectly well in the refrigerator, becoming light and fragrant.
When the dough has risen, top with tomatoes, and arrange the Gorgonzola (at room temperature) on top. Let the pizza rise for 40 minutes more. Bake at 425°F (220°C) for 20 minutes, or until the cheese is bubbly and the crust is golden brown. Sprinkle the walnuts on top.

PIZZA WITH MUSHROOMS
AND HAM

Preparation time: 15 minutes   Rising time: 1 1/2–6 hours
Cooking time: 15 minutes   Difficulty: medium

4 SERVINGS

FOR THE DOUGH
4 cups (500 g) **all-purpose flour** or
Italian "00" flour, plus more as needed
1 1/2 cups (350 ml) **lukewarm water**
1 1/2 tbsp. (20 ml) **extra-virgin olive oil**
1 1/2 tsp. (4 g) **active dry yeast** for
2-hour rising time, or 3/4 tsp. (2 g)
for 6-hour rising time
2 tsp. (12 g) **salt**

FOR THE TOPPING
1 16-oz. can **peeled tomatoes**, crushed
by hand
14 oz. (400 g) **mozzarella cheese**, finely
sliced
10 **button mushrooms**, sliced, or about
8 oz.
7 thin slices of **ham**

Put the flour onto a clean work surface and make a well in the center. Dissolve the yeast in the water, and pour the yeast mixture into the well. Gradually start incorporating the yeast mixture into the flour until a loose dough starts to form, then add the oil and salt. Knead the dough until smooth and elastic. Rub the dough with a little oil, cover with plastic wrap, and let it rest for about 10 minutes. Grease a 12-inch round pizza pan with oil. Transfer the dough to the pan and, using your fingertips, spread the dough to cover the bottom of the pan. If you used 1 1/2 tsp. of yeast, let the dough rise for about 40 minutes. If you used 3/4 tsp. yeast, then cover dough with lightly oiled plastic wrap and refrigerate for at least 5 hours. The dough will rise well in the refrigerator, becoming light and fragrant. When the dough has risen, top it with tomatoes, mozzarella and mushrooms (all at room temperature) on top. Let the pizza rise 40 minutes more. Bake at 425°F (220°C) for 18 minutes. Add the ham and bake for 2 minutes more, or until the cheese is bubbly and the crust is golden brown.

PEPPERONI PIZZA

Preparation time: 15 minutes   Rising time: 1 1/2–6 hours
Cooking time: 20 minutes   Difficulty: medium

4 SERVINGS

FOR THE DOUGH
4 cups (500 g) **all-purpose flour** or
Italian "00" flour, plus more as needed
1 1/2 cups (350 ml) **lukewarm water**
1 1/2 tbsp. (20 ml) **extra-virgin olive oil**
1 1/2 tsp. (4 g) **active dry yeast** for
2-hour rising time, or 3/4 tsp. (2 g)
for 6-hour rising time

2 tsp. (12 g) **salt**

FOR THE TOPPING
1 16-oz. can **peeled tomatoes**, crushed
by hand
14 oz. (400 g) **mozzarella cheese**, thinly
sliced
20 **slices spicy pepperoni sausage**

Put the flour onto a clean work surface and make a well in the center. Dissolve the
yeast in the water, and pour the yeast mixture into the well. Gradually start
incorporating the yeast mixture into the flour until a loose dough starts to form,
then add the oil and salt. Knead the dough until smooth and elastic. Rub the
dough with a little oil, cover with plastic wrap, and let it rest for about 10 minutes.
Grease a 12-inch round pizza pan with oil. Transfer the dough to the pan and,
using your fingertips, spread the dough to cover the bottom of the pan.
If you used 1 1/2 tsp. of yeast, let the dough rise for about 40 minutes. If, on the
other hand, you used 3/4 tsp., then cover the dough with a sheet of lightly oiled
plastic wrap and refrigerate for at least 5 hours. The dough will rise perfectly well
in the refrigerator, becoming light and fragrant.
When the dough has risen, spread the tomatoes over it, and arrange the
mozzarella and the pepperoni (all at room temperature) on top.
Let the pizza rise for another 40 minutes. Bake in the oven at 425°F (220°C) for 20
minutes, or until the cheese is bubbly and the crust is golden brown.

MARINARA PIZZA

Preparation time: 15 minutes   Rising time: 1 1/2–6 hours
Cooking time: 20 minutes   Difficulty: medium

4 SERVINGS

FOR THE DOUGH
4 cups (500 g) **all-purpose flour** or
Italian "00" flour, plus more as needed
1 1/2 cups (350 ml) **lukewarm water**
1 1/2 tbsp. (20 ml) **extra-virgin olive oil**
1 1/2 tsp. (4 g) **active dry yeast** for
2-hour rising time, or 3/4 tsp. (2 g)
for 6-hour rising time

2 tsp. (12 g) salt

FOR THE TOPPING
1 16-oz. can **peeled tomatoes**, crushed
by hand
3 cloves **garlic**, thinly sliced

Put the flour onto a clean work surface and make a well in the center. Dissolve the
yeast in the water, and pour the yeast mixture into the well. Gradually start
incorporating the yeast mixture into the flour until a loose dough starts to form,
then add the oil and salt. Knead the dough until smooth and elastic. Rub the
dough with a little oil, cover with plastic wrap, and let it rest for about 10 minutes.
Grease a 12-inch round pizza pan with oil. Transfer the dough to the pan and, using
your fingertips, spread the dough to cover the bottom of the pan.
If you used 1 1/2 tsp. of yeast, let the dough rise for about 40 minutes. If, on the
other hand, you used 3/4 tsp., then cover the dough with a sheet of lightly oiled
plastic wrap and refrigerate for at least 5 hours. The dough will rise perfectly well in
the refrigerator, becoming light and fragrant.
When the dough has risen, spread the peeled tomatoes (at room temperature)
evenly over it. Let the pizza rise for another 40 minutes. Bake at 425°F (220°C) for 20
minutes, or until the cheese is bubbly and the crust is golden brown. As soon as it
comes out of the oven, sprinkle garlic on top.

NEAPOLITAN PIZZA

Preparation time: 30 minutes   Rising time: 1 1/2 hours–5 hours
Cooking time: 8 minutes   Difficulty: medium

4 SERVINGS

FOR THE DOUGH
5 cups (650 g) **all-purpose flour** or
Italian "00" flour, plus more as needed
1 1/2 cups (375 ml) lukewarm water
1 1/2 tsp. (4 g) **active dry yeast** for
2-hour rising time, or 3/4 tsp. (2 g)
for 5-hour rising time
3 tsp. (18 g) **salt**

FOR THE TOPPING
7 oz. (200 g) **tomato purée**
14 oz. (400 g) **tomatoes** (preferably
beefsteak or other ribbed variety),
sliced or diced
1 lb. 2 oz. (500 g) **buffalo mozzarella**,
thinly sliced
1/2 **bunch fresh basil**
Extra-virgin olive oil
Salt

Put flour onto a clean work surface; make a well in the center. Dissolve yeast in
the water. Gradually incorporate into flour until a loose dough forms; add salt.
Knead dough until smooth. Cover with lightly oiled plastic wrap and let rise until
doubled in volume (from 1 to 4 hours, depending on the temperature).
Divide the dough into four portions and roll them into balls. Let them rise again until
again doubled in size (from 30 minutes to 1 hour, depending on the temperature).
Flour work surface; flatten each ball, starting with your fingertips and progressing
to a rotary movement of your hands as the dough gets flatter and wider, into a
round about 8 inches in diameter. Put the rounds on a baking sheet.
Season the tomato purée with salt and a dash of olive oil, and spread it over
each dough round. Top with mozzarella and tomatoes. Bake at 480°F (250°C) for
8 minutes, or until the cheese is bubbly and the crust is golden brown. Garnish
with the basil leaves.

APULIAN-STYLE PIZZA

*Preparation time: 15 minutes   Rising time: 1 1/2–6 hours
Cooking time: 20 minutes   Difficulty: medium*

4 SERVINGS

FOR THE DOUGH
4 cups (500 g) **all-purpose flour** or
Italian "00" flour, plus more as needed
1 1/2 cups (350 ml) **lukewarm water**
1 1/2 tbsp. (20 ml) **extra-virgin olive oil**
1 1/2 tsp. (4 g) **active dry yeast** for
2-hour rising time, or 3/4 tsp. (2 g)
for 6-hour rising time
2 tsp. (12 g) **salt**

FOR THE TOPPING
1 16-oz. can **peeled tomatoes**, crushed
by hand
2 **yellow onions**
10 **green and black olives**, sliced
7 **slices Caciocavallo** or provolone
cheese
Fresh oregano (optional)

Put the flour onto a clean work surface and make a well in the center. Dissolve the
yeast in the water, and pour the yeast mixture into the well. Gradually start
incorporating the yeast mixture into the flour until a loose dough starts to form,
then add the oil and salt. Knead the dough until smooth and elastic. Rub the
dough with a little oil, cover with plastic wrap, and let it rest for about 10 minutes.
Grease a 12-inch round pizza pan with oil. Transfer the dough to the pan and, using
your fingertips, spread the dough to cover the bottom of the pan.

If you used 1 1/2 tsp. of yeast, let the dough rise for about 40 minutes. If, on the
other hand, you used 3/4 tsp., then cover the dough with a sheet of lightly oiled
plastic wrap and refrigerate for at least 5 hours. The dough will rise perfectly well in
the refrigerator, becoming light and fragrant.

When the dough has risen, top it with tomatoes, the Caciocavallo or provolone,
onions, and olives (all at room temperature). Let rise for 40 minutes more. Bake at
425°F (220°C) for 20 minutes, or until the cheese is bubbly and the crust is golden
brown. Garnish with oregano.

ROMAN-STYLE PIZZA

Preparation time: 15 minutes Rising time: 1 1/2–6 hours
Cooking time: 20 minutes Difficulty: medium

4 SERVINGS

FOR THE DOUGH
4 cups (500 g) **all-purpose flour** or
Italian "00" flour, plus more as needed
1 1/2 cups (350 ml) **lukewarm water**
1 1/2 tbsp. (20 ml) **extra-virgin olive oil**
1 1/2 tsp. (4 g) **active dry yeast** for
2-hour rising time, or 3/4 tsp. (2 g)
for 6-hour rising time
2 tsp. (12 g) **salt**

FOR THE TOPPING
1 16-oz. can **peeled tomatoes**, crushed
by hand
14 oz. (400 g) **mozzarella cheese**, finely
sliced
8 **anchovies in oil**, drained
10 **capers**

Put the flour onto a clean work surface and make a well in the center. Dissolve
the yeast in the water, and pour the yeast mixture into the well. Gradually start
incorporating the yeast mixture into the flour until a loose dough starts to form,
then add the oil and salt. Knead the dough until smooth and elastic. Rub the
dough with a little oil, cover with plastic wrap, and let it rest for about 10 minutes.
Grease a 12-inch round pizza pan with oil. Transfer the dough to the pan and,
using your fingertips, spread the dough to cover the bottom of the pan.
If you used 1 1/2 tsp. of yeast, let the dough rise for about 40 minutes. If, on the
other hand, you used 3/4 tsp., then cover the dough with a sheet of lightly oiled
plastic wrap and refrigerate for at least 5 hours. The dough will rise perfectly well
in the refrigerator, becoming light and fragrant.
When the dough has risen, spread the tomatoes over it and top with the
mozzarella, anchovies and capers (all at room temperature). Let it rise for 40
minutes more. Bake at 425°F (220°C) for 20 minutes, or until the cheese is bubbly
and the crust is golden brown.

PIZZA WITH EGG

Preparation time: 30 minutes   Rising time: 1 1/2 hours–5 hours
Cooking time: 2-8 minutes   Difficulty: medium

4 SERVINGS

FOR THE DOUGH
5 cups (650 g) **all-purpose flour**
1 1/2 cups (375 ml) **lukewarm water**
3/4 tsp. (2 g) **active dry yeast**
1 tbsp. (18 g) **salt**

FOR THE TOPPING
1 lb 5 oz. (600 g) **crushed tomatoes**
1 lb 2 oz. (500 g) **mozzarella**, *thinly
sliced*
4 large **eggs**
Dried oregano
Extra-virgin olive oil
Salt *to taste*

Put the flour onto a clean work surface and make a well in the center. Dissolve the yeast in the water, and pour into well. Gradually incorporate into the flour until a loose dough forms; add the salt. Knead dough until smooth. Cover with lightly oiled plastic wrap and let rise until doubled in volume (from 1 to 4 hours, depending on the temperature). Divide the dough into four portions and roll them into balls. Let them rise again until they have again doubled in size (from 30 minutes to 1 hour, depending on the temperature).

Season the tomatoes with salt, a pinch of oregano, and a drop of oil. Sprinkle the work surface with flour and flatten each dough ball, starting with your fingertips and progressing to a rotary movement of your hands as the dough gets flatter and wider, into a round about 8 inches in diameter. Put the dough rounds on a baking sheet.

Preheat oven to 480°F (250°C). Spread the crushed tomatoes over the pizzas and top with mozzarella. Crack an egg onto the middle of each pizza.

Bake for 7 to 8 minutes, or until cheese is bubbly and the crust is golden brown.

ROMAN-STYLE PIZZA
WITH CACIOTTA AND CAPOCOLLO

Preparation time: 30 minutes   Rising time: 1 1/2 hours–5 hours
Cooking time: 8 minutes   Difficulty: medium

4 SERVINGS

FOR THE DOUGH
5 cups (650 g) **all-purpose flour** or
Italian "00" flour, plus more as needed
1 1/2 cups plus 1 tsp. (375 ml)
lukewarm water
3/4 tsp. (2 g) **active dry yeast**
1 tbsp. (18 g) **salt**

FOR THE TOPPING
1 1/3 lbs (600 g) **crushed tomatoes**
9 oz. (250 g) **Roman Caciotta-style** (or
Manchego) cheese, thinly sliced
4 1/4 oz. (120 g) **Capocollo** (cured pork
cold cut)
Oregano to taste
Extra-virgin olive oil
Salt to taste

Put flour onto a clean work surface; make a well in the center. Dissolve yeast in the
water; pour into well. Gradually incorporate into flour until a loose dough forms; add
salt. Knead dough until smooth and elastic. Cover dough with oiled plastic wrap and
let rise until it doubles in volume (from 1 to 4 hours, depending on the temperature).
Divide the dough into four portions and roll them into balls. Let them rise again,
covered with lightly oiled plastic wrap, until they again double in size (from 30
minutes to 1 hour depending on the temperature).

Season the tomatoes with salt and a dash of olive oil.

Flour work surface and flatten each dough ball, progressing from using fingertips
to a rotary movement of your hands as the dough gets flatter and wider, into a
round about 8 inches in diameter. Put the rounds on a baking sheet.

Spread the tomatoes over pizzas, and top with the Caciotta, half the Capocollo
and oregano to taste. Bake at 480°F (250°C) for 8 minutes, or until the cheese is
bubbly and the crust is golden brown. Garnish with the remaining Capocollo.

PIZZA WITH EGGPLANT
AND PROVOLA CHEESE

Preparation time: 30 minutes   Rising time: 1 1/2 hours–5 hours
Cooking time: 8 minutes   Difficulty: medium

4 SERVINGS

FOR THE DOUGH
5 cups (650 g) **all-purpose flour** or
Italian "00" flour, plus more as needed
1 1/2 cups plus 1 tsp. (375 ml)
lukewarm water
3/4 tsp. (2 g) **active dry yeast**
1 tbsp. (18 g) **salt**

FOR THE TOPPING
1 lb (500 g) **crushed tomatoes**
1 lb (500 g) **Sicilian Provola** (or Fontina
or Pecorino) cheese, thinly sliced
10 1/2 oz. (300 g) **eggplant**
9 oz. (250 g) **Pachino** or cherry tomatoes
Extra-virgin olive oil
Salt to taste

Put the flour onto a clean work surface and make a well in the center. Dissolve the yeast in the water, and pour it into the well. Gradually incorporate into the flour until a loose dough forms, then add the salt. Knead the dough until smooth and elastic. Cover the dough with lightly oiled plastic wrap and let rise until it doubles in volume (from 1 to 4 hours, depending on the temperature).
Divide the dough into four portions and roll them into balls. Let them rise again, covered with lightly oiled plastic wrap, until they again double in size (from 30 minutes to 1 hour, depending on the temperature).
Season the crushed tomatoes with salt and a dash of olive oil. Slice and grill the eggplant, or fry the slices in olive oil, then drain. Halve the tomatoes.
Sprinkle the work surface with flour and flatten each dough ball, starting with your fingertips and progressing to a rotary movement of your hands as the dough gets flatter and wider, into a round about 8 inches in diameter. Put the rounds on a baking sheet. Spread the crushed tomatoes over the pizzas and top with the cheese, tomatoes and eggplant. Bake at 480°F (250°C) for 8 minutes, or until the cheese is bubbly and the crust is golden brown.

PIZZA WITH BACON AND POTATO

Preparation time: 30 minutes   Rising time: 1 1/2 hours–5 1/2 hours
Cooking time: 8 minutes   Difficulty: medium

4 SERVINGS

FOR THE DOUGH
5 cups (650 g) **all-purpose flour** or
Italian "00" flour, plus more as needed
1 1/2 cups plus1 tbsp. (375 ml)
lukewarm water
3/4 tsp. (5 g) **active dry yeast**
1 tbsp. (18 g) **salt**

FOR THE TOPPING
1/3 lb (150 g) **sliced bacon**
2/3 lb (300 g) **potatoes**
2 **sprigs fresh rosemary**, chopped
Extra-virgin olive oil
Salt to taste

Put the flour onto a clean work surface and make a well in the center. Dissolve the yeast in the water, and pour it into the well. Gradually incorporate into the flour until a loose dough forms, then add the salt. Knead the dough until smooth and elastic. Cover the dough with lightly oiled plastic wrap and let rise until it doubles in volume (from 1 to 4 hours depending on the temperature).

Divide the dough into four portions and roll them into balls. Let them rise again, covered with lightly oiled plastic wrap, until they again double in size (from 30 minutes to 1 hour depending on the temperature).

Wash, peel, and finely slice the potatoes.

Sprinkle the work surface with flour and flatten each dough ball, starting with your fingertips and progressing to a rotary movement of your hands as the dough gets flatter and wider, into a round about 8 inches in diameter. Put rounds on a baking sheet. Arrange the bacon and potato on top of the pizzas and sprinkle with the rosemary, a pinch of salt and a drizzle of olive oil.

Bake at 480°F (250°C) for 8 minutes, or until the potatoes and crust are golden brown.

PIZZA WITH LEEKS,
SAUSAGE AND CHEESE

Preparation time: 30 minutes   Rising time: 1 1/2 hours–5 1/2 hours
Cooking time: 8 minutes   Difficulty: medium

4 SERVINGS

FOR THE DOUGH
5 cups (650 g) **all-purpose flour** or
Italian "00" flour, plus more as needed
1 1/2 cups plus 1 tsp. (375 ml)
lukewarm water
3/4 tsp. (2 g) **active dry yeast**
1 tbsp. (18 g) **salt**

FOR THE TOPPING
1 1/3 lbs (600 g) **crushed tomatoes**
14 oz. **fresh pork sausage**, finely chopped
7 oz. (200 g) **Bra Tenero** or Cheddar
cheese, diced
2 **leeks**, white parts only, sliced
Extra-virgin olive oil
Salt to taste

Put the flour onto a clean work surface and make a well in the center. Dissolve
the yeast in the water, and pour the yeast mixture into the well. Gradually start
incorporating the yeast mixture into the flour until a loose dough starts to form,
then add the salt. Knead the dough until smooth and elastic. Cover the dough
with lightly oiled plastic wrap and let rise in a warm room until it has doubled in
volume (it can take from 1 to 4 hours depending on the temperature).
Form dough into four balls. Let rise again until they again double in size
(from 30 minutes to 1 hour).
Season the crushed tomatoes to taste with salt and olive oil.
Sprinkle the work surface with plenty of flour and flatten each dough ball with
your hands, starting with your fingertips and progressing to a rotary movement
of your hands as the dough gets flatter and wider, into a round about 8 inches in
diameter. Put the dough rounds on a baking sheet.
Spread the crushed tomatoes evenly over the pizzas. Arrange the cheese,
sausage and leeks on top. Bake at 480°F (250°C) for about 8 minutes, or until
cheese is bubbly and the crust is golden brown.

PIZZA WITH PARMA HAM

Preparation time: 15 minutes   Cooking time: 20 minutes
Rising time: 2–6 hours   Difficulty: medium

4 SERVINGS

FOR THE DOUGH
4 cups (500 g) **all-purpose flour** or
Italian "00" flour, plus more as needed
1 1/2 tsp. (4 g) **active dry yeast** for
2-hour rising time, or 3/4 tsp. (2 g)
for 6-hour rising time
1 1/2 cups (350 ml) **lukewarm water**
1 1/2 tbsp. (20 ml) **extra-virgin olive oil**
2 tsp. (12 g) **salt**

FOR THE TOPPING
1 16-oz. can **peeled tomatoes**, crushed
by hand
14 oz. (400 g) **mozzarella cheese**, thinly
sliced
10 thin slices **Parma ham**

Put the flour onto a clean work surface and make a well in the center. Dissolve the yeast in the water, and pour it into the well. Gradually incorporate into the flour until a loose dough forms, then add the oil and salt. Knead the dough until smooth and elastic. Rub the dough with a little oil, cover with plastic wrap, and let it rest for about 10 minutes. Oil a 12-inch round pizza pan. Using your fingertips, spread the dough to cover the bottom of the pan.

If you used 1 1/2 teaspoons of yeast, let the dough rise for about 40 minutes. If you used 3/4 tsp. teaspoons of yeast, then cover the dough with lightly oiled plastic wrap and refrigerate for at least 5 hours. The dough will rise well in the refrigerator, becoming light and fragrant.

When the dough has risen, top with tomatoes and mozzarella (at room temperature). Let it rise 40 minutes more. Bake at 425°F (220°C) for 20 minutes, or until the cheese is bubbly and the crust is golden brown. Top with ham (at room temperature).

PIZZA WITH ARUGULA
AND PARMIGIANO-REGGIANO CHEESE

Preparation time: 15 minutes   Cooking time: 20 minutes
Rising time: 2–6 hours   Difficulty: medium

4 SERVINGS

FOR THE DOUGH
4 cups (500 g) **all-purpose flour** or
Italian "00" flour, plus more as needed
1 1/2 cups (350 ml) **lukewarm water**
1 1/2 tbsp. (20 ml) **extra-virgin olive oil**
1 1/2 tsp. (4 g) **active dry yeast** for
2-hour rising time, or 3/4 tsp. (2 g)
for 6-hour rising time
2 tsp. (12 g) **salt**

FOR THE TOPPING
1 16-oz. can **medium peeled
tomatoes,** crushed by hand
14 oz. (400 g) **mozzarella cheese,** thinly
sliced
4 oz. (113 g) **baby arugula,** chopped
5 1/4 oz. (150 g) fresh-grated
Parmigiano-Reggiano cheese

Put the flour onto a clean work surface and make a well in the center. Dissolve the
yeast in the water, and pour the yeast mixture into the well. Gradually start
incorporating the yeast mixture into the flour until a loose dough starts to form,
then add the oil and salt. Knead the dough until smooth and elastic. Rub the
dough with a little oil, cover with plastic wrap, and let it rest for about 10 minutes.
Grease a 12-inch round pizza pan with oil. Transfer the dough to the pan and
using your fingertips, spread the dough to cover the bottom of the pan.
If you used 1 1/2 teaspoons of yeast, let the dough rise in a warm room for about
40 minutes. If, on the other hand, you used 3/4 teaspoon of yeast, then cover the
dough with lightly oiled plastic wrap and refrigerate for at least 5 hours. The
dough will rise perfectly well in the refrigerator, becoming light and fragrant.
When the dough has risen, spread the tomatoes over it, and top with the
mozzarella (at room temperature). Let it rise 40 minutes more. Bake at 425°F
(220°C) for 20 minutes or until the crust is golden brown.
Garnish with the arugula and Parmigiano-Reggiano (at room temperature).

PIZZA WITH SPECK
AND SMOKED SCAMORZA CHEESE

Preparation time: 15 minutes   Rising time: 2–6 hours
Cooking time: 20 minutes   Difficulty: medium

4 SERVINGS

FOR THE DOUGH
4 cups (500 g) **all-purpose flour** or
Italian "00" flour, plus more as needed
1 1/2 cups (350 ml) **lukewarm water**
1 1/2 tbsp. (20 ml) **extra-virgin olive oil**
1 1/2 tsp. (4 g) **active dry yeast** for
2-hour rising time, or 3/4 tsp. (2 g)
for 6-hour rising time
2 tsp. (12 g) **salt**

FOR THE TOPPING
1 16-oz. can **peeled tomatoes**, crushed
by hand
14 oz. (400 g) **mozzarella cheese**
10 **slices speck**
6 **slices smoked Scamorza** or smoked
mozzarella cheese, thinly sliced

Put the flour onto a clean work surface and make a well in the center. Dissolve the yeast in the water, and pour the yeast mixture into the well. Gradually start incorporating the yeast mixture into the flour until a loose dough starts to form, then add the oil and salt. Knead the dough until smooth and elastic. Rub the dough with a little oil, cover with plastic wrap, and let it rest for about 10 minutes. Grease a 12-inch round pizza pan with oil. Transfer the dough to the pan and using your fingertips, spread the dough to cover the bottom of the pan. If you used 1 1/2 teaspoons of yeast, let the dough rise in a warm room for about 40 minutes. If, on the other hand, you used 3/4 teaspoon of yeast, then cover the dough with lightly oiled plastic wrap and refrigerate for at least 5 hours. The dough will rise perfectly well in the refrigerator, becoming light and fragrant. When the dough has risen, spread the tomatoes evenly on the pizzas. Arrange the mozzarella, speck and smoked Scamorza (all at room temperature) on top. Let the pizza rise for another 40 minutes and then bake in the oven at 425°F (220°C) for about 20 minutes, or until cheese is bubbly and crust is golden brown.

PIZZA WITH SPINACH
AND RICOTTA CHEESE

Preparation time: 30 minutes   Rising time: 1 1/2 hours-5 1/2 hours
Cooking time: 8 minutes   Difficulty: medium

4 SERVINGS

FOR THE DOUGH
5 cups (650 g) **all-purpose flour** or
Italian "00" flour, *plus more as needed*
1 1/2 cups plus 1 tsp. (375 ml)
lukewarm water
3/4 tsp. (2 g) **active dry yeast**
2 1/2 tsp. (18 g) **salt**

FOR THE TOPPING
1 lb (500 g) **ricotta cheese**
1 lb (500 g) **fresh spinach**
1 oz. (30 g) **Parmigiano-Reggiano
cheese**, *grated*
1 clove **garlic**
3 tbsp. (45 ml) **extra-virgin olive oil**

Put the flour onto a clean work surface and make a well in the center. Dissolve
the yeast in the water, and pour it into the well. Gradually incorporate into the
flour until a loose dough forms, then add the salt. Knead the dough until smooth
and elastic. Cover the dough with lightly oiled plastic wrap and let rise until
doubled in volume (from 1 to 4 hours, depending on the temperature).
Divide the dough into four portions and roll them into balls. Let them rise again,
covered with lightly oiled plastic wrap, until again doubled in size (from 30
minutes to 1 hour, depending on the temperature).
Brown the garlic in the olive oil. Wash and drain the spinach, then sauté it lightly
in the same skillet over high heat. Add salt to taste. Discard garlic.
Sprinkle the work surface with plenty of flour and flatten each dough ball,
starting with your fingertips and progressing to a rotary movement of your hands
as the dough gets flatter and wider, into a round about 8 inches in diameter. Put
rounds on a baking sheet. Mound the spinach and the ricotta over pizzas.
Sprinkle with the Parmigiano-Reggiano. Bake at 480°F (250°C) for about 8
minutes, or until the cheese is bubbly and the crust is golden brown.

PIZZA MARGHERITA

Preparation time: 15 minutes *Rising time: 2–6 hours*
Cooking time: 20 minutes *Difficulty: medium*

4 SERVINGS

FOR THE DOUGH
4 cups (500 g) **all-purpose flour** or
Italian "00" flour, plus more as needed
1 1/2 cups (350 ml) **lukewarm water**
1 1/2 tbsp. (20 ml) **extra-virgin olive oil**
1 1/2 tsp. (4 g) **active dry yeast** for
2-hour rising time, or 3/4 tsp. (2 g)
for 6-hour rising time

2 tsp. (12 g) **salt**

FOR THE TOPPING
1 16-oz. can **peeled tomatoes**, crushed
by hand
14 oz. (400 g) **mozzarella cheese**, thinly
sliced
1/2 **bunch fresh basil**

Put the flour onto a clean work surface and make a well in the center. Dissolve the
yeast in the water, and pour the yeast mixture into the well. Gradually start
incorporating the yeast mixture into the flour until a loose dough starts to form,
then add the oil and salt. Knead the dough until smooth and elastic. Rub the
dough with a little oil, cover with plastic wrap, and let it rest for about 10 minutes.
Grease a 12-inch round pizza pan with oil. Transfer the dough to the pan and
using your fingertips, spread the dough to cover the bottom of the pan.
If you used 1 1/2 teaspoons of yeast, let the dough rise in a warm room for about
40 minutes. If, on the other hand, you used 3/4 teaspoon of yeast, then cover the
dough with lightly oiled plastic wrap and refrigerate for at least 5 hours. The
dough will rise perfectly well in the refrigerator, becoming light and fragrant.
When the dough has risen, spread the peeled tomatoes over it. Top with
mozzarella (at room temperature). Let it rise 40 minutes more. Bake at 425°F
(220°C) for 20 minutes, or until the cheese is bubbly and the crust is golden brown
Garnish with fresh basil leaves.

SFINCIONE
SICILIAN PIZZA

Preparation time: 30 minutes   Rising time: 1 1/2 hours
Cooking time: 25 minutes   Difficulty: medium

4 SERVINGS

FOR THE DOUGH
2 cups (250 g) **durum wheat flour** *or semolina flour*
2 cups (250 g) **all-purpose flour** *or Italian "00" flour, plus more as needed*
2 1/4 tsp. (6 g) **active dry yeast**
1 cup (250 ml) **lukewarm water**
1 1/4 tsp. (5 g) **sugar**
3 tbsp. plus 1 tsp. (50 ml) **extra-virgin olive oil**
2 tsp. (12 g) **salt**

FOR THE TOPPING
3 **medium tomatoes**, *peeled, seeded and finely chopped*
8 **anchovies**, *desalted or in oil*
3 1/2 oz. (100 g) **fresh Caciocavallo** *or provolone cheese*
3 1/2 oz. (100 g) **semi-seasoned Caciocavallo** *or provolone cheese, grated*
1 medium **onion**, *finely chopped*
3 tbsp. plus 1 tsp. (50 ml) **extra-virgin olive oil**
Salt and pepper to taste
Chopped fresh oregano

Mix the flours on a clean work surface and make a well in the center. Dissolve the yeast in the water and add it to the well. Gradually incorporate into the flour until a loose dough forms. Add the sugar and the oil and, lastly, the salt dissolved in 3 tbsp. (50 ml) of water. Knead the dough until smooth and elastic. Cover the dough with lightly oiled plastic wrap and let rise until doubled in volume, about 1 hour. In a bowl, toss the tomatoes with the salt, pepper and oil. Stir in the onion and a pinch of oregano.
Spread the dough with your fingertips in a greased round baking pan. Cover it with the cheese, the anchovies, and the tomato mixture. Let it rise for at least 30 minutes. Bake at 450°F (230°C) for 25 minutes, or until crust is golden brown and cheese is melted.

FOCACCIA

The history of focaccia, that quieter sister of pizza, is lost in the mists of time. It would appear that an ancestor of focaccia was made by the Phoenicians, the Carthaginians, and the Greeks with barley, millet, or rye flour. It was no more than bread, seasoned with fat, cooked over a fire. Indeed, the name *focaccia* derives from the Latin word *focus*, which means hearth or fire pan. But whereas bread is a necessity, focaccia is a treat. In ancient Rome, it was offered to the gods, and during the Renaissance, it was served at wedding banquets.

Liguria is the Italian region that, more than any other, has made focaccia a famous local product. The Genovese focaccia is more than two centimeters high, crusty on the surface but soft on the inside and topped with extra-virgin olive oil from Liguria. In some places, the surface has a thin layer of sliced raw onion, or a sprinkling of pepper and rosemary, or scented fennel seeds. In yet others, chopped green or black olives and sage leaves are incorporated.

Novi focaccia is a Piedmontese specialty, made in a nonindustrial manner in the bakeries of Novi Ligure and Ovada. It looks like Genoese focaccia but differs from it in that it is thinner (at most 1/2 inch or 1 cm thick) and is seasoned with less extra-virgin olive oil.

Even in southern Italy, a tradition has developed to season focaccia in different ways. The best known is the focaccia from Apulia, traditionally eaten at Sunday picnics. The topping of cherry tomatoes and oregano make this rustic focaccia similar to a pizza, while the potatoes in the dough render it soft and give it a special taste.

Be creative!

Focaccia can also be made with cereals other than wheat; for example, Khorasan wheat, corn, or spelt. You can even use buckwheat flour, which is not a "true" grass but which is used traditionally in Trentino and Lombardy for making bread. There are focaccias to suit all tastes. Focaccia made with polenta or chickpea flour is delicious. Alternatively, you can add wine or beer to the focaccia dough. And then you can season it in an infinite number of ways: with Genoese pesto sauce, potatoes, and green beans, with chopped herbs in the dough, even topped with onions or with olives and Robiola cheese. Of course, focaccia can also lend itself to sweet preparations. It is a great idea for brunch.

BORLENGO
(CRÊPE)

Preparation time: 10 minutes   Rising time: 1 hour
Cooking time: 5 minutes   Difficulty: medium

4 SERVINGS

2 cups (250 g) **all-purpose flour** or cake flour
4 1/4 cups (1 l) **lukewarm water**
1 tbsp. (18 g) **salt**
1 **egg**
2 tbsp. (30 g) **unsalted butter**
1 3/4 oz. (50 g) **lard** or bacon fat
1 **spring fresh rosemary**
1 clove **garlic**
3 1/2 oz. (100 g) **Parmigiano-Reggiano cheese**, grated

Whisk together the flour, the water and the egg. Add the salt last and whisk until a smooth batter forms.
Let the batter rest at room temperature for at least 1 hour.
Meanwhile, finely chop together the lard or bacon fat with the rosemary and garlic.
Heat a 9- to 10-inch nonstick skillet or a crêpe pan greased with a little butter over medium heat (traditionally a copper pan greased with ham rind was used).
Pour a ladle (about 1/4 cup) of batter into the hot pan, tilting evenly to coat bottom. Cook until underside is set and lightly browned, about 45 seconds. Flip the crêpe with a rubber spatula and cook for about 30 seconds more.
Sprinkle the center of each borlengo with the mixture of bacon fat and herbs, then sprinkle with the Parmigiano-Reggiano.
Fold in half, then in half again and serve immediately.

VEGETABLE CALZONE

Preparation time: 30 minutes   Rising time: 1 1/2 hours–5 1/2 hours
Cooking time: 8 minutes   Difficulty: medium

4 SERVINGS

FOR THE DOUGH
5 cups (650 g) **all-purpose flour** or
Italian "00" flour, plus more as needed
1 1/2 cups plus 1 tsp. (375 ml)
lukewarm water
3/4 tsp. (2 g) **active dry yeast**
2 1/2 tsp. (18 g) **salt**

FOR THE FILLING
1 lb (500 g) **tomatoes**, or about 5 medium
10 1/2 oz. (300 g) **peppers**, or about 2
1/2 medium
1 3/4 oz. (50 g) **spring onions**
7 oz. (200 g) **eggplant**
7 oz. (200 g) **spinach**
1/2 **bunch fresh basil**, chopped
1/2 cup (100 ml) **extra-virgin olive oil**
Salt to taste

Put flour onto a clean work surface; make a well in the center. Dissolve yeast in the
water; pour into well. Gradually incorporate into flour until a loose dough forms;
add the salt. Knead dough until smooth. Cover dough with oiled plastic wrap and
let rise until doubled in volume (from 1 to 4 hours, depending on the temperature).
Divide dough into four portions and roll them into balls. Let dough portions rise
again, covered with lightly oiled plastic wrap, until again doubled in size (from 30
minutes to 1 hour depending on the temperature). Wash and chop spinach. Cut
vegetables into a 1-inch (2 cm) dice and fry separately, in olive oil, with salt to
taste, until crisp. Put vegetables and basil in a bowl, stir, and let cool.
On a floured work surface, flatten each dough ball, starting with your fingertips
and progressing to a rotary movement of your hands as the dough gets flatter and
wider, into a round about 8 inches in diameter. Put rounds on a baking sheet.
Spread vegetables over half of each disk, fold in half and seal edges. Bake at
500°F (250°C) for 8 minutes, or until crust is golden brown.

CRESCIONE
WITH BEET GREENS

Preparation time: 30 minutes   Rising time: 1 hour
Cooking time: 8 minutes   Difficulty: medium

4 SERVINGS

FOR THE DOUGH	FOR THE FILLING
4 cups (500 g) **all-purpose flour**	*1 lb. (500 g)* **beet greens**
or cake flour	*1 oz. (30 g)* **Parmigiano-Reggiano cheese**
1/2 cup (125 ml) **lukewarm milk**	*7/8 oz. (25 g)* **lard** or bacon fat, softened
1 large **egg**	*1 tbsp. plus 2 tsp. (25 ml)* **extra-virgin**
2 2/3 oz. (75 g) **lard** or bacon fat, softened	**olive oil**
1 tbsp. (15 g) **baking powder**	*1 clove* **garlic**
1 2/3 tsp. (10 g) **salt**	**Salt and pepper** to taste

Put the flour onto a clean work surface and make a well in the center. Add the milk, egg, baking powder, lard, and salt to the well and mix to blend. Gradually blend into the flour, and then begin to knead. Continue kneading the dough until smooth and elastic.

Cover the dough with a kitchen towel and let rest for at least 1 hour.

Prepare the beet greens; cut, wash, drain and sauté them in a pan with the lard or bacon fat (or olive oil) and garlic. Add salt and pepper. Cook for 5 minutes. Discard garlic. Let the greens cool, chop them coarsely and mix in the Parmigiano-Reggiano.

Divide the dough into small loves, of 5 oz. (150 grams) each. Roll them out into discs of about 1/8 inch (3 mm) thick and 10 to 12 inches (25 to 30 cm) in diameter. Put some of the cooked greens in the middle of each disc, fold in half and seal the edges.

Cook the crescioni on a greased griddle or in a nonstick pan over high heat for 4 minutes on each side, or until golden brown and the cheese has melted.

CRESCIONE
WITH PORCINI MUSHROOMS AND CHEESE

Preparation time: 30 minutes   Rising time: 1 hour
Cooking time: 8 minutes   Difficulty: medium

4 SERVINGS

FOR THE DOUGH
4 cups (500 g) **all-purpose flour** or
Italian "00" flour
3/4 cup plus 2 tbsp. (200 ml) **milk**
1 large **egg**
2 2/3 oz. (75 g) **lard**
1 tbsp. (15 g) **baking powder**
1 1/2 tsp. (10 g) **salt**

FOR THE FILLING
10 1/2 oz. (300 g) **porcini mushrooms**,
cleaned and diced into 1-inch cubes
4 1/4 oz. (120 g) **soft cheese**, such as
Trachino or Crescenza, diced
1 tbsp plus1 tsp. (20 ml) **extra-virgin
olive oil**
1 clove **garlic**
1 tbsp. (4 g) **parsley**

Put flour onto a clean work surface; make a well in the center. Add milk, egg, baking powder, lard, and salt to the well; blend. Gradually incorporate mixture into flour. Knead dough until soft, smooth, and elastic.
Cover the dough with a kitchen towel and let rest for at least 1 hour.
Heat the oil in a skillet. Add the mushrooms and garlic and sauté briefly. Stir in the parsley, salt and pepper to taste, and sauté for 5 minutes, or until the mushrooms are softened. Remove from heat and let cool. Discard the garlic.
Divide the dough into small loaves of about 5 oz. (150 grams) each. Roll them out into discs of about 1/8 inch (3 mm) thick and 10 to 12 inches (25 to 30 cm) in diameter. Put some of the cooked mushrooms in center of each disc with some cheese. Fold the disks in half and seal the edges.
Cook the crescioni on a greased griddle or in a nonstick pan over high heat for 4 minutes on each side, or until golden brown and the cheese has melted.

BEER FOCACCIA

Preparation time: 20 minutes   Rising time: 2 1/2 hours
Cooking time: 20 minutes   Difficulty: medium

4 SERVINGS

FOR THE DOUGH
4 cups (500 g) **all-purpose flour**
or cake flour
1 1/3 cup (300 ml) **lukewarm beer**
1 tbsp. (15 ml) **extra-virgin olive oil**
2 1/4 tsp. (6 1/2 g) **active dry yeast**
1 1/2 tsp. (10 g) **salt**

FOR THE GENOESE BRINE
3 1/2 tbsp. (50 ml) **water**
1 tbsp. plus 2 tsp. (25 ml) **extra-virgin
olive oil**
1 1/4 tsp. (7 g) **coarse salt**

Put the flour onto a clean work surface, mix the yeast into the flour and make a
well in the center. Pour the the beer into the well and gradually start
incorporating it into the flour a little at a time. Add the oil and, lastly, the salt,
and knead the dough until it is soft, smooth and elastic.
Cover the dough with a sheet of lightly oiled plastic wrap and let rise in a warm
place until it has doubled in size (about 1 hour).
To make the brine, combine the water, olive oil and coarse salt in a bowl. Stir to
make an emulsion and then let it rest.
Roll out the dough to a thickness of about 1/3 inch (1 cm) and transfer it to a
round, lightly oiled baking pan. Let it rest for another 10 minutes, then gently
spread out the dough with your fingertips to cover the base of the pan.
Sprinkle the focaccia with the brine, smearing it over the surface with your
hands, and prod the dough with your fingers to form small dimples where the
seasoning will collect. Let it rise in a warm place for 90 minutes.
Bake at 390°F (200°C) for about 20 minutes, or until golden brown.

SAGE FOCACCIA

Preparation time: 15 minutes   *Rising time: 1 1/2 hours*
Cooking time: 25 minutes   *Difficulty: medium*

4 SERVINGS

FOR THE FOCACCIA
4 cups (500 g) **all-purpose flour**
1 1/2 tsp. (4 g) **active dry yeast**
1 cup (250 ml) **lukewarm water**
1 tbsp. (10 g) **malt** or 1/2 tbsp. (10 g)
honey
10 **sage leaves**, finely chopped
2 tbsp. plus 2 tsp. (40 ml) **extra-virgin
olive oil**

1 1/2 tsp. (10 g) **salt**

FOR THE GENOESE BRINE
1/2 cup (100 ml) **water**
3 tbsp. plus 1 tsp. (50 ml) **extra-virgin
olive oil**
2 1/4 tsp. (14 g) **coarse salt**

Put the flour onto a clean work surface and make a well in the center. Dissolve
the yeast in the water. Pour the yeast mixture and malt into the well, and
gradually start incorporating them into the flour a little at a time. Add the sage
and oil. Lastly, add the salt and knead the dough until soft, smooth and elastic.
Cover the dough with a sheet of lightly oiled plastic wrap and let rise in a warm
place for about 30 minutes.
To make the brine, combine the water, olive oil and coarse salt in a bowl. Stir to
make an emulsion and then let it rest.
Transfer the dough to a lightly oiled baking pan, stretching it gently with your
fingertips. Prod the surface of the dough with your fingers, forming small
dimples where the seasoning will collect. Sprinkle the focaccia with the brine and
let rise until it has doubled in volume, about 1 hour.
Bake at 390°F (200°C) for about 25 minutes, or until golden brown.

ONION FOCACCIA

Preparation time: 20 minutes   Rising time: 1 1/2 hours
Cooking time: 20 minutes   Difficulty: medium

4 SERVINGS

4 cups (500 g) **all-purpose flour**
or cake flour
1 cup plus 2 tbsp. (270 ml) **lukewarm**
water
2 1/2 tsp. (10 g) **sugar**
2 tbsp. plus 2 tsp. (40 ml) **extra-virgin**
olive oil
1 1/2 tsp. (4 g) **active dry yeast**
1 1/2 tsp. (10 g) **salt**

FOR THE GENOESE BRINE
1 tbsp. plus 2 tsp. (25 ml) **water**
3 tbsp. (45 ml) **extra-virgin olive oil**
1/2 tbsp. (8 g) **coarse salt**

FOR THE TOPPING
12 oz. (350 g) **onions,** *or about 2*
medium, thinly sliced

Put the flour onto a clean work surface, make a well in the center, and add the sugar. Dissolve the yeast in the water. Pour the yeast mixture into the well, and gradually start incorporating it into the flour a little at a time. Add the oil and lastly, add the salt. Knead the dough until soft, smooth, and elastic.

Cover the dough with a sheet of lightly greased plastic wrap and let rise in a warm place for about 30 minutes.

To make the brine, combine the water, olive oil, and coarse salt in a bowl. Stir to make an emulsion and then let it rest.

In a lightly oiled baking pan, stretch the dough gently with your fingertips. Prod the surface of the dough with your fingers, forming small dimples where the seasoning will collect. Sprinkle the focaccia with the brine and let rise until it has doubled in volume, about 1 hour.

In a large skillet, sauté the onions in a little olive oil until softened. Spread onions over the focaccia.

Bake at 390°F (200°C) for 20 minutes, or until golden brown.

FOCACCIA WITH OLIVES
AND ROBIOLA CHEESE

Preparation time: 25 minutes   Rising time: 1 1/2 hours
Cooking time: 25 minutes   Difficulty: medium

4 SERVINGS

4 cups (500 g) **all-purpose flour**
1 cup plus 2 tbsp. (270 ml) **lukewarm water**
1 tbsp. (10 g) malt or 1/2 tbsp. (10 g) **honey**
2 tbsp. plus 2 tsp. (40 ml) **extra-virgin olive oil**
1 1/2 tsp. (4 g) **active dry yeast**
1 1/2 tsp. (10 g) **salt**

FOR THE GENOESE BRINE
1/2 cup (100 ml) **water**
3 tbsp+1 tsp. (50 ml) **extra-virgin olive oil**
2 1/4 tsp. (14 g) **coarse salt**

FOR THE FILLING AND GARNISH
1 1/4 cups (300 g) **fresh Robiola cheese**
1/2 cup (100 g) **pitted olives**

Put flour onto a clean work surface; make a well in the center. Dissolve yeast in water. Pour it, plus the malt, into the well. Gradually incorporate into flour. Add the oil and salt. Knead dough until smooth. Cover with oiled plastic wrap; let rise for 30 minutes. To make the brine, combine the water, olive oil, and coarse salt in a bowl. Stir to make an emulsion and then let it rest.

In a greased baking pan, stretch dough gently with your fingertips. Prod dough surface with your fingers, forming dimples where the seasoning will collect. Sprinkle focaccia with brine and let rise until doubled in volume, about 1 hour. Scatter olives on focaccia. Bake at 390°F (200°C) for 25 minutes, or until golden brown.

When focaccia is cool, divide into equal portions. Soften Robiola cheese by stirring it with a dash of oil. Spread on half of focaccia. Top with other half; cut into slices.

SPELT FOCACCIA

Preparation time: 15 minutes   Rising time: 1 1/2 hours
Cooking time: 25 minutes   Difficulty: medium

4 SERVINGS

5 cups (500 g) **spelt flour**
1 cup (250 ml) **lukewarm water**
1 tbsp. (10 g) **malt** or 1/2 tbsp. (10 g)
honey
2 tbsp. plus 2 tsp. (40 ml) **extra-virgin
olive oil**
1 tbsp. plus 3/4 tsp. (11 g) **active
dry yeast**
1 1/2 tsp. (10 g) **salt**

FOR THE GENOESE BRINE
1/2 cup (100 ml) **water**
3 tbsp plus 1 tsp. (50 ml) **extra-virgin
olive oil**
3/4 tbsp. (14 g) **coarse salt**

Put the flour onto a clean work surface, make a well in the center, and add the malt. Dissolve the yeast in the water. Pour the yeast mixture into the well, and gradually start incorporating it into the flour a little at a time. Add the oil and lastly, add the salt. Knead the dough until soft, smooth, and elastic.
Cover the dough with a sheet of lightly greased plastic wrap and let rise in a warm place for about 30 minutes.
To make the brine, combine the water, olive oil, and coarse salt in a bowl. Stir to make an emulsion and then let it rest.
In a lightly oiled baking pan, stretch the dough gently with your fingertips. Prod the surface of the dough with your fingers, forming small dimples where the seasoning will collect. Sprinkle the focaccia with the brine and let rise until doubled in volume, about 1 hour.
Bake in the oven at 390°F (200°C) for about 25 minutes, or until golden brown.

FOCACCIA FROM NOVI LIGURE

Preparation time: 15 minutes   Rising time: 1 1/2 hours
Cooking time: 20 minutes   Difficulty: medium

4 SERVINGS

4 cups (500 g) **all-purpose flour** *or cake flour*
1 cup plus 1 1/2 tbsp. (275 ml) **lukewarm water**
1/2 tbsp. (5 g) **malt**
1 tbsp. plus 2 tsp. (25 ml) **extra-virgin olive oil**
1 1/2 tbsp. (20 g) **lard**, *softened*

1 3/4 tsp. (5 g) **active dry yeast**
1 2/3 tsp. (10 g) **salt**

FOR THE GENOESE BRINE
1/2 cup (100 ml) **water**
3 1/2 tbsp. (50 ml) **extra-virgin olive oil**
3/4 tbsp. (14 g) **salt**

Put the flour onto a clean work surface, make a well in the center, and add the malt. Dissolve the yeast in the water. Pour mixture into the well, and gradually incorporate into the flour. Add the softened lard, the oil and, lastly, add the salt. Knead the dough until soft, smooth, and elastic. Cover the dough with a sheet of lightly oiled plastic wrap and let rise for about 1 hour.

To make the brine, combine the water, olive oil, and coarse salt in a bowl. Stir to make an emulsion and then let it rest.

Transfer the dough to a baking pan greased with oil, stretching it gently with your fingertips until it is about 1/2 inch (1 cm) thick. Prod the surface of the dough with your fingers, forming small dimples where the seasoning will collect. Sprinkle the focaccia with the Genoese brine and let it rise for half an hour. Bake at about 450°F (230°C) for 20 minutes, or until golden brown. Brush the surface of the freshly baked focaccia with olive oil.

FOCACCIA FROM APULIA

Preparation time: 15 minutes Rising time: 1 1/2 hours
Cooking time: 20 minutes Difficulty: medium

4 SERVINGS

4 cups (500 g) **all-purpose flour**
1 cup (170 g) **semolina flour**
1 2/3 cups (400 ml) **lukewarm water**
1/4 cup plus 1 tsp. (65 ml) **extra-virgin olive oil**
2 1/4 tbsp. (6 g) **active dry yeast**
2 1/2 tsp. (15 g) **salt**

3 oz. (80 g) **potatoes**, or about 1 1/2 small
FOR THE TOPPING
7 oz. (200 g) **cherry tomatoes**, halved
Dried regano
Olive oil
Coarse salt

Put the potatoes in a saucepan and cover with cold water. Bring to a boil and cook until tender, about 15 minutes. Drain the potatoes, let cool slightly and then mash them.

Combine the two types of flours on a clean work surface and make a well in the center. Dissolve the yeast in 1 cup (240 ml) of the lukewarm water. Pour the yeast mixture into the well, and gradually start incorporating it into the flour a little at a time. Add the salt, oil, mashed potatoes, and the remaining water, little by little. Knead the dough until soft, smooth, and elastic.

Divide the dough into 4 balls. Place each ball of dough in a well-oiled 8-inch round baking pan and let rise in a warm place for about 3 hours.

Once the first rising is done, flip the dough pieces over and spread each with your fingertips to cover the bottom of the pan. Top each with the tomatoes, a pinch of salt, a little olive oil, and oregano.

Let them rise again until doubled in volume, about 30 minutes.

Bake in the oven at 430°F (220°C) for 25 minutes, or until golden brown.

CORN FOCACCIA

Preparation time: 15 minutes   Rising time: 2 hours
Cooking time: 20 minutes   Difficulty: medium

4 SERVINGS

4 cups (500 g) **all-purpose flour** or cake flour
2 cups (200 g) **cornmeal**
2 2/3 cups (380 ml) **lukewarm water**
1 1/2 tbsp. (10 g) **sugar**
2 tsp. (10 ml) **extra-virgin olive oil**
1 tbsp. plus 3/4 tsp. (10 g) **active dry yeast**
2 tsp. (12 g) **salt**

Mix the flour and the cornmeal together on a clean work surface, make a well in the center and add the sugar. Dissolve the salt in 2 tablespoons of water. Dissolve the yeast in the remaining water. Pour the yeast mixture into the well, and gradually start incorporating it into the flour a little at a time. Add the oil and lastly, add the salt mixture. Continue to knead until the dough is soft, smooth and elastic.
Cover the dough with a sheet of lightly oiled plastic wrap and let rise in a warm place until it has doubled in volume (about 1 hour).
Divide the dough into 4 pieces and, using your hands, roll each piece into a rope, then flatten it with your fingers.
Transfer to a lightly oiled baking sheet and sprinkle the surface with a pinch of cornmeal flour. Let the dough rise for 30 minutes in a warm place.
Bake the little focaccias in the oven at 450°F (230°C) for about 20 minutes, or until golden brown.

BUCKWHEAT FOCACCIA

Preparation time: 15 minutes   Rising time: 2 hours
Cooking time: 20 minutes   Difficulty: medium

4 SERVINGS

*3 5/8 cups (400 g) **all-purpose flour** or cake flour*
*2 cups (250 g) **buckwheat flour***
*1 1/2 cups (350 ml) **lukewarm water***
*2 tsp. (10 ml) **extra-virgin olive oil***
*1 tbsp. plus 3/4 tsp. (25 g) **active dry yeast***
1 2/3 tsp. (10 g) salt

Combine the two types of flour on a clean work surface and make a well in the center. Dissolve the salt in 2 tablespoons of the water. Dissolve the yeast in the remaining water. Pour the yeast mixture into the well, and gradually start incorporating it into the flour a little at a time. Add the salt mixture and the oil little by little. Knead the dough until soft, smooth, and elastic.
Cover the dough with a sheet of lightly oiled plastic wrap and let rise in a warm place until it has doubled in volume (about 1 hour).
Divide the dough into 4 pieces and form each piece into a ball.
Place balls of dough on a lightly oiled baking pan and flatten them with your fingers. Let them rise in a warm place for about 1 hour.
Bake at 450°F (230°C) for about 20 minutes, or until golden brown.

CHICKPEA FOCACCIA

Preparation time: 30 minutes   Rising time: 2 hours
Cooking time: 20 minutes   Difficulty: medium

4 SERVINGS

FOR THE DOUGH
3 cups (375 g) **all-purpose flour** or cake flour
1 1/3 cups (125 g) **chickpea flour**
1 2/3 cups (280 ml) **lukewarm water**
1 tbsp. (10 g) **malt**
2 1/4 tsp. (10 ml) **extra-virgin olive oil**

1 tbsp. (8 g) **active dry yeast**
1 1/2 tsp. (10 g) **salt**

FOR THE TOPPING
3 1/2 tbsp. (50 ml) **extra-virgin olive oil**
Pepper to taste

Mix together the two types of flour on a clean work surface and make a well in the center. Dissolve the salt in 3 tablespoons of water. Dissolve the yeast in the remaining water. Pour the yeast mixture into the well, and gradually start incorporating it into the flour a little at a time. Add the malt and the oil and, lastly, the salt mixture. Knead the dough until soft, smooth and elastic.
Cover the dough with a sheet of lightly oiled plastic wrap and let rise in a warm place until it has doubled in volume (about 1 hour).
Divde the dough into 4 balls. Place them in a lightly oiled baking pan and let rise in a warm place for about 30 minutes.
Flatten the dough into disks. Prod the surface of the dough with your fingers, forming small dimples where the seasoning will collect. Brush the surface with oil and sprinkle with fresh coarsely ground pepper. Let the focaccia rise for another 30 minutes.
Bake in the oven at 420°F (220°C) for about 20 minutes, or until golden brown.

PANZEROTTO FROM APULIA

Preparation time: 30 minutes   Rising time: 1 1/2 hours
Cooking time: 5 minutes   Difficulty: medium

4 SERVINGS

FOR THE DOUGH
2 cups (250 g) **all-purpose flour** or
Italian type "00" flour
1 1/8 cups (280 ml) **lukewarm water**
1 tbsp. plus 3/4 tsp. (10 g) **active dry yeast**
1 1/2 tsp. (10 g) **salt**
Vegetable oil for frying

FOR THE FILLING
4 1/4 oz. (150 g) **tomatoes**, peeled and chopped
10 1/2 oz. (300 g) **mozzarella cheese**, diced
1 3/4 oz. (50 g) **Parmigiano-Reggiano cheese**, grated
1/4 cup (55 ml) **extra-virgin olive oil**
4 **fresh basil leaves**
1 clove **garlic**, finely chopped
Salt and pepper to taste

Put the flour onto a clean work surface, make a well in the center. Dissolve the yeast in the water. Pour into the well, and gradually incorporate it into the flour. Add the salt. Knead the dough until smooth and elastic. Cover the dough with a sheet of lightly oiled plastic wrap and let rise until doubled in size (about 1 hour). Meanwhile, heat the olive oil in a pan and sauté garlic. Add the chopped tomatoes, salt and pepper. Cook for about 20 minutes or until the sauce thickens. Divide the dough into balls of about 3 1/2 ounces (100 g) each and let them rise again until they have doubled in size (about 30 minutes). Roll out the dough into disks. Spread the tomato sauce on half of each disk. Arrange a basil leaf on each, and sprinkle with mozzarella and Parmigiano-Reggiano. Fold the disks in half and seal the edges.
Heat 1/2 inch of oil in a large skillet until hot and shimmering. Fry the panzerotti for about 5 minutes, until brown on both sides. With a slotted spoon, transfer the panzerotti to paper towels to drain. Add salt to taste.

PIADINA
WITH EXTRA-VIRGIN OLIVE OIL

Preparation time: 10 minutes   Rising time: 1 hour
Cooking time: 5 minutes   Difficulty: easy

4 SERVINGS

4 cups (500 g) **all-purpose flour** *or cake flour*
1/2 cup (125 ml) **lukewarm water**
3 tbsp. plus 1 tsp. (50 ml) **extra-virgin olive oil**
1 tbsp. (15 g) **baking powder**
1 1/2 tsp. (10 g) **salt**

Put the flour on a clean work surface and make a well in the center. Add the water, baking powder, oil, and salt, and gradually start incorporating them into the flour a little at a time. Knead the dough until smooth and elastic.
Cover the dough with a kitchen towel and let rise for at least 1 hour.
Divide the dough into pieces about 5 ounces(150 grams) each. Shape them into balls, then roll them out into disks of about 1/8 inch (3 mm) thick and 10 to 12 inches (25 to 30 cm) in diameter.
Cook the disks on both sides on a greased griddle or in a nonstick pan over high heat until golden brown. As the piadina cooks, a few bubbles will form on the surface; prick them with a fork.

CLASSIC PIADINA

Preparation time: 10 minutes   *Rising time: 1 hour*
Cooking time: 5 minutes   *Difficulty: easy*

4 SERVINGS

4 cups (500 g) **all-purpose flour** *or cake flour*
7/8 cup (200 ml) **milk**
1 large **egg**, *lightly beaten*
2 2/3 oz. (75 g) **lard**, *softened and diced*
3 tsp. (15 g) **baking powder**
1 2/3 tsp. (10 g) **salt**

Sift the flour with the baking powder, then place the mixture on a clean work surface and make a well in the center. Scatter the small pieces of lard, along with the salt, over the flour mixture. Pour the egg and the milk into the well and gradually start incorporating them into the flour mixture a little at a time. Knead the dough until smooth and elastic.

Cover the dough with a kitchen towel and let rise for at least 1 hour.

Divide the dough into small loaves of about 5 oz. (150 g) each. Roll them out into disks of the desired thickness, usually around 1/8 inch (3 mm), and 10 to 12 inches (25 to 30 cm) in diameter.

Cook the disks on both sides on a greased griddle or in a nonstick pan over high heat until golden brown. As the piadina cooks, a few bubbles will form on the surface; prick them with a fork.

Note: Although the traditional recipe for piadina calls for lard, using extra-virgin olive oil instead yields a lighter, crispier result.

INGREDIENTS INDEX

PHOTO CREDITS

· · · · · · · · · · · ·

The Taunton Press, Inc.
63 South Main Street
PO Box 5506, Newtown, CT 06470-5506
e-mail: tp@taunton.com

Translations:
Catherine Howard - Mary Doyle - John Venerella - Free z'be, Paris
Salvatore Ciolfi - Rosetta Translations SARL - Rosetta Translations SARL

LIBRARY OF CONGRESS CATALOGING-IN-PUBLICATION DATA IN PROGRESS
ISBN: 978-1-62710-053-3

Printed in China
10 9 8 7 6 5 4 3 2 1